24 EASY CLASSICAL

SOLOS FOR CELLO

HARRY HUNT, JR., MFA

A2G
ENTERTAINMENT, INC.

24 Easy Classical Solos for Cello
Harry Hunt, Jr., MFA

Published by A2G Entertainment Inc.
Chicago, IL
harryhuntjr.com

ISBN: 978-1-954127-44-9 (Paperback)

Printed in the USA
Third Edition

CONTENTS

PLAY-ALONG & DEMONSTRATION TRACKS

To Stream or Download

Click or Visit

harryhuntjr.net/book-ecs-cello

OTHER LINKS

https://sites.google.com/view/book-tracks/cello

(bookmark the links in your browser for quicker access)

1. HOT CROSS BUNS

(Two-bar piano intro)

2. LIGHTLY ROW

(Two-bar piano intro)

3. LULLABY

Brahms

(Two-bar piano intro - pickup starts on beat 3)

4. AU CLAIR DE LA LUNE

(Two-bar piano intro)

5. TWINKLE

(Two-bar piano intro)

6. SCARBOROUGH FAIR

(Two-bar piano intro)

7. OH SUSANNA

Foster

(Two-bar piano intro - pickup starts on beat four)

8. MARRIAGE OF FIGARO

Mozart

(Two-bar piano intro)

9. LONG LONG AGO

Bayly

(Two-bar piano intro)

10. RONDEAU

Mouret

(Two-bar piano intro - pickup starts on beat four)

11. PIANO CONCERTO #3

Beethoven

(Two-bar piano intro)

12. SYMPHONY #7 (2nd Movement)

Beethoven

(Two-bar piano intro)

13. GERMAN DANCE

Mozart

(Two-bar piano intro)

14. CHORAL FANTASY

Beethoven

(Two-bar piano intro - pickup starts on beat two)

15. THE HEAVENS ARE TELLING

Haydn

(Two-bar piano intro - pickup starts on beat four)

16. BOURRÉE (Water Music)

Handel

(Two-bar piano intro - pickup starts on beat four)

17. CARNIVAL OF VENICE

Benedict

(Two-bar piano intro - pickup starts on beat three)

18. SONATINA #1

Beethoven

(Two-bar piano intro)

19. LONDONDERRY AIR

(Two-bar piano intro - pickup starts on beat two)

20. BLUE DANUBE

Strauss

(Two-bar piano intro - pickup starts on beat three)

21. MINUET I

(Two-bar piano intro)

Bach

22. EINE KLEINE

Mozart

(Two-bar piano intro)

23. SYMPHONY #7 (3rd Movement)

Beethoven

(Two-bar piano intro - pickup starts on beat three)

24. MINUET

Bach

(Two-bar piano intro)

Made in the USA
Middletown, DE
29 November 2025

23530195R00015